Author's notes:

Thank you for taking the time out to read my works. Please understand that life is what we make it. The color of your skin does not make you a bad person or a good person, only you can do that. When you look in the mirror every day and you hate the person that you see looking back at you, make changes for the better. If your entire life is in shambles, stand strong, relax and regroup. Help is you. How did you become this individual? Who are your ancestors? What is your history? With the knowledge that is provided to us on the internet and inside these influential books authors have written, we no longer have excuses. Your situation does not determine your future. Prepare to be better. Strive for success. Never give up.

PROLUGE

We seek answers to stop the violence in the black community but we are not ready to receive that knowledge. As a group of people, a unit, it is crucial to clean our own environments up. We know our "hoods" better than anyone else. Police, military enforcement, or the government cannot help us more than we can help ourselves. Let us clean it up. Complaining about the next person killing one of our Black American's and calling it an act of racism can seem quite ignorant when we kill one another on a daily basis merely because of the color of our skin.

Are we racist to our own as well? When the home boy from down the street is killed by the home boy around the corner, because of drugs, gangs, robbery, or just because, that is not racist? In the root of all black on black crime is self-hate, racism against your own people. Wake up! We pulled the trigger for George Zimmerman, as well as gave him the get out of jail free card!

Our lives have become worthless. How much does a black soul go for now a days? Our brothers, sons and husbands are losing their lives Due to gang violence, violent robberies, drugs, and all around ignorance. When will we stop using our privilege of being ignorant to what is going on around us? When will we begin to educate ourselves with life's knowledge versus "hood" knowledge? When will we actually begin to live instead of just surviving? That is a question I ask my young brothers and my old brothers.

Sisters stand up! We are the black man's downfall. Enablers, ready to mend every broken heart as if we are not broken ourselves. Pockets broken, hearts broken and spirit broken women are mending hearts and nurturing at any level they can just for love, love from self-hating individuals. Love yourself enough for the both of you! Push that man but never carry him, you may be strong enough but he will break you if he gets the chance. Stand firm and deliver. Be a queen and nothing less. Demand greatness from your husband, son and father. Never settle!

We have to build our communities back up. The time is now. NO MORE TRAYVON'S! SAVE OUR SONS!

Dope Fiends and Dope Friends

"You stupid bitch! I wanted a fucking Tahitian treat not no damn Mountain dew, take y'all funky asses back to the store and get my shit. Y'all aint going no damn where and where my ten dollas Lisa?" Said Ms. Brenda.

She was facing Lisa but her statement was to the both of us.

Lisa mom was crazy as hell. It was the same mess every time. We had to go get her crazy ass mom something to drink and a pack of cigarettes while she chilled with her friends. She made us do this or Lisa would not be able to leave the house.

"Momma, alright. Dang!" Lisa screamed at her mom handing her a ten dollar bill as we were leaving out of the house.

"Dude yo momma be tripped out." I whispered getting into the car.

"Tell me about it. You gone take me to get this pop?" She asked.

"Yea I got you. I don't want her to beat my ass." I responded in laughter to soften the moment.

I drove her to the corner store; it was about 30 seconds away driving and 2 minutes away walking. She was in an out. The only thing going through my head was the game. It started in thirty minutes and my boyfriend was playing so I had to get there on time or he would have choice words for me afterwards.

When we pulled back up to the house I hopped out first.

"You don't have to go in, I'll go." Lisa said when I got out of the car.

"Naw, yo momma gonna make us do something else crazy if you go in there. I'll go alone this time." I responded.

"You might be right. Be careful, she in there with her friends and they be doing the most." She replied.

"Girl, I am not scared of your momma and her friends. I will kick some crusty as if I need to." I responded reassuring her that I would be fine.

"Don't touch my momma and don't say I didn't tell you." She screamed out the window as I knocked on the door.

One of Ms. Brenda's friends answered the door. She had one shoe on the left foot, and not even a sock on the right one. The right foot was so ashy and infected looking. She needed to comb her hair three days ago the way it was all over her head, it was matted on one side and sticking up on the other, and I could smell vomit as she spoke.

"You aint Lisa daughter." She said when she answered the door.

"I'm her friend. Where is Ms. Brenda? I have her pop." I said in a snappy tone.

The lady was rubbing me the wrong way and I did not have a clue who she was.

"Oh chile gimme that. I will give it to her." She said grabbing towards the soda pop bottle I was holding.

"ummm, that's okay I can give it to her myself." I responded pushing the door open all the way and walking through.

I could not even stomach listening, well smelling the woman talk anymore. She looked like she needed the drink more than Ms. Brenda so giving it to her was not an option. I would handle this task on my own.

"Ms. Brenda!" I yelled walking through the house.

The woman followed me mumbling the entire time. I opened doors and shut them looking for Ms. Brenda and the heffa not once offered to help.

Lisa and her mom lived in a two family flat that had been condensed to a one family home. The house was huge but the up keep was terrible.

You could tell that her mom did not care if the house was cleaned, or the dishes were washed.

The stove looked like it had food on it since Christmas time, and that was 4 months ago.

Her home dynamic was much different than mines. My parents would be screaming at me for the dishes looking like that, not some cigarettes and a soda pop.

Finally, after searching through the large home I found Ms. Brenda in one of the upstairs rooms off to the side of the second staircase.

"Ms. Brenda!" I yelled walking into the smoke filled room.

She was smoking her cigarette on the couch in the far back. Ms. Brenda was having a party, well it seemed like it. By the amount of people I saw in the room if she was not having a party she needed to be charging those people rent.

When I first walked in the room I could see the man on the left cutting his toe nails and eating them. I could not help but to think that that was some foul mess that should be done in the privacy of his own home.

The lady sitting next to Ms. Brenda barely had on any clothes. She had the nerve to be wearing a dirty, sweaty looking sports bra that used to be white and some jeans that she needed to either wash or toss in the garbage. They were discolored with food stains all over them.

I handed Ms. Brenda the Tahitian treat. My mind was going a million miles per hour trying to figure out what the hell was going on. Everybody in that room either looked crazy, was acting crazy, or all of the above.

"Thank you, you okay with me you little bitch." Responded Ms. Brenda.

"Thanks, I think." I responded as I started out the door.

I looked down on the floor and noticed a used pipe. Quickly I glanced over the rest of the floor that was visible and saw what looked to be a syringe and miscellaneous items such as small plastic bags, beer bottles, cheap liquor bottles and pill containers. I turned to look at Ms. Brenda but she had disappeared in the smoke.

Leaving out of the room, I could not help but to think that Ms. Brenda was not just a chain smoking alcoholic, and her friends that looked beat out of shape were not just "friends" of Ms. Brenda.

When I finally got outside Lisa was getting out of the car.

"Girl what the hell took you so long in there?" She responded to my timely trip into her home.

"Yo momma crazy ass friend wouldn't even let me in, and then she wouldn't tell me where your mom was. I had to look around the house for her like a serial killer. I found her though. She was in that backroom. I did not know all of those people were inside your house, it be like this all the time?" I asked with a serious inquire.

"Hell yea. That's why I be at Mike house or at work all the damn time. Shit I be on time to school every day." She replied.

Mike was Lisa's boyfriend and he was the shit. I mean dude took care of her like she was his kid. We all went to school together our first two years of high School but Mike was a two years older than us. He made sure Lisa stayed in the finest and the girl had no car but she never needed a ride. Either she was driving his car, his mom car or she could easily be dropped off. My boyfriend did not have anything on Mike.

"Damn, girl I got mad respect for you. My momma would be getting a piece of my mind every day."

She laughed, "Yea, and the fact that every time I come home something else is missing out of my room."

"What you mean?" I responded as we headed to the game.

"Shit. My momma and she cracked out ass friends be all in my stuff. Last week I had $350.00 under my pillow. I got home from school and it was gone. I was sick." She replied as if it was nothing.

"What! $350. I would've punched my momma in her damn throat." I responded pissed off as if it was my money.

"You funny as hell, my momma crazy as fuck when she on that shit, she be clean for like three months out of the year though. I will wait until her sober days to tell her about all the fucked up shit she done did to me all of the other 9 months out of the year. I'm just hoping she clean for Christmas, ya know?" She asked casually but this was not a casual matter, or was it?

In that moment I asked myself, how many of my friends was really dealing with this craziness? And if there was anything that could be done about these parents that choose drugs over their children.

"What I do know is that you should've been told me that was why yo crazy ass momma stayed cussing me out every time I called your house phone, or that's the reason she always making us go get cigarettes and charging you ten dollars to leave the house." I responded

"Man I don't be wanting no sympathy. Mike and you are the only friends that I trust with this. I know yo mean ass won't treat me any differently, plus you been taking the cuss outs like a true G. Shit she aint yo momma, I might've cussed yo momma smooth out for the shit." She said laughing.

Lisa was admirable in that moment. She laughed and smiled through her trials because they were a way of life. I would forever remember this moment. Just the thought of her strength and her courage was sure to bring me out of my darkest times.

What Changed Black?

We had our Sojourner Truth's

Our Martin Luther King's

Now we have our Brenda's

Yes she has a baby

Our Nate Abrams

The adolescent murderer

Stand for something ladies

Sara Baartman took that fall

Stand for something men

Your jail bed is made at 7 years old

3rd grade test scores imprisoning my sons

Stand for something my people

Fight for advancement

Crack and jail, crack and jail

Black and ghetto, Black and ghetto

Stand for something dammit!

Black Boy Illiterate

He dunked that

Moved the ball across his waist

Slammed it all through the nets

The crowd went cray

Your grades came back son

I passed this time

Yes son this season should be fun

Everyone grew quiet

They stared in awe

He came crashing down as if he had tried to fly

The game was no longer about the ball

A year later laced up

No shoes, just crazy moods

I cannot do shit fuck!

Trayvon Martin Lives to Tell a Story

"Ted!" Velma screamed.

"Yea!!" Ted screamed back.

"Boy who you talking to like that, get your narrow behind up these stairs and put that game controller down before I give you something to scream about". I said to my 12 year old son Theodore.

Ted will spend all of his home hours either playing video games alone or playing tournaments with his friends if I let him.

"Yes momma." He said sounding defeated. His head dangled to the side and his facial expression simultaneously shared his annoyance. I held in my laughter as I took in the visual of my son −my little man, and saw a younger version of my husband staring me in the face.

"Boy why are you looking like that? That game is not that important. Did you read the articles that I left on the table for you?" I asked.

I knew the answer already so I prepared myself for the partial lie, quivered lip, stuttering and everything else my child would soon come up with.

"Yeah. I liked it too. I was confused about why he was killed but it was cool to read an article about someone that was the same age as me, he dressed like me and he was killed for those same reasons. Not that I think it is cool that he is dead but Ma, he killed him for no reason. It is a different type of feeling." He said. He showed no emotion at all.

My dramatics wanted my emotions to overpower the moment and coerce me to drop a tear, but not today— I was a proud mother once again.

"Well smack me twice and call me a bitch four times! I just knew you were going to tell me how you didn't see the articles, and thought I was going to have to persuade you to go and read them with a short report." I said.

He burst out laughing and I joined him as I padded the empty spot next to me motioning for him to have a seat.

"Ma I aint never heard nothing like that before in my life. That junk is crazy. Dude just shot him cuz he thought he was a criminal? I mean I go to the store around the corner all the time and people steal stuff but the owner don't be trying to shoot us every time we walk in there." He responded anxiously.

"Well baby haven't you ever noticed the way the women at the mall over there in Auburn Hills? How they switch their purses to the other side when walking next to you or your daddy?" I asked curious to hear his answer.

"Not really, never paid any attention to those women. I wonder have pops noticed." He said.

I could tell that he was in deep thought while he tried to remember an incident of such and wondering about his father's past.

"I've discussed these things with your father before, and he has experienced these things just the same". I enlightened him.

"But why? I mean I and Justin play together all the time, his mom and dad is cool too." He said confused.

"That's the thing baby, all people don't think the same. You just have to be aware of the ones that think a certain way. Never feel that all white people are judging you and treating you badly; there are many white people that will respect you and treat you as a human. Some white people will never find your ethnicity as a handicap or relate it to criminology." I responded.

"Well that man thought the boy in the article was a criminal for no reason it seem like. All because of a hoodie, he thought the boy had a gun?" He asked.

"You're right. Exactly why I needed you to read that article." I said.

"So how can I tell who's bad or, who's good?" He asked.

"There is no bad or good, you have to find out what they think about you, their understanding of who you are." I responded.

"But they don't know me they just think they do." He acknowledged.

"Son you might be smarter than you look." I said in an attempt to lighten the moment.

Ted really related to the article about young Trayvon Martin.

"Ma, I'm way smarter than I look, maybe from all the video games I play." He laughed.

He was probably replaying one of my video game rants through his head. They would usually end with him storming to his room and me following behind taking controllers as if he didn't have a computer to play the games on as well.

"Now you're losing your marbles again I see. Well you can go back to your video games since I rudely or shall I say motherly interrupted. Just promise me that you will keep the article in mind."

"What!? I'm telling everybody to read it even Justin. People need to know what is going on, that wasn't right. It may be the way some people think but that don't mean they should think like that mom." He said excited and frustrated at the same time.

"Honey I couldn't have said that any better. I'm proud of you and your little rock head. Soon I'm going to be reading published articles you have written." I responded.

"Oh no. I am going to either design video games, play basketball, or play football professionally." He said very sure of himself.

"Well athlete maybe you should spend a little less time playing those video games and more time practicing catching a ball, running, or shooting a ball. Just maybe though." I said in a sarcastic tone.

I know that my son is bright and talented enough to do whatever he put his mind to, but I also know how lazy and short his attention span is as well.

"I hear you." He was actually listening.

Tomorrow, after school, he is going to have all of his little friends in the driveway playing basketball.

I shoved him playfully motioning for him to get out of my face and back to his video game. All I can think about is how lucky I am to have a son like him. We are going to be alright. My son will not be the stereotypical black man, going to jail, or walking around with a chip on his shoulder. Instead he will grow up having an understanding of how people portray him, giving him the tools to communicate effectively with others that don't look like him and possibly are not used to people that look like him.

Trayvon Martin

George Zimmerman I could kill you myself

Up in Texas with your hood on

Got Mrs. Zimmerman screaming for help

Pathetic gun handler

Coward little bitch

My son will know you meddler

Coward little prick

Your hood stood behind you

My hood got me killed

America America America America fucking boo

Anger we shouldn't feel?

Fuck you!

Lady's Night

Friday night was hanging out night. After a long work week and an even longer school week, my girls and I had to escape the madness and let our hair down. Hang out nights usually consisted of heavy drinking and smoking, somebody fighting or cursing somebody out, hitting up a club or two, and bringing the after party back to our apartment.

"I bought vodka, tequila, and hen. Bitches drink up." Shonda sang as she walked through the door. She put the bags of liquor on the table and lined them up perfect for pouring shots.

Shonda was my girl. I met her my freshman year of college. We had a speech class together. Being one of the only blacks that went to the university, we clicked quickly. After knowing her for a few weeks, we started hanging out at all of the school functions together. She lived on campus, I commuted. Her living on campus came in handy; I would spend the night in her dorm when I had an early class or a late night.

You know those late nights that you knew your parents would kick your ass for. "Coming in the crib at 5 or 6 in the morning like you grown." My momma would say.

Now, even in our last year of college we were still hanging tough, partying just as hard but working ten times harder.

"Damn, you trying to black out tonight huh?" I asked pulling the tequila out and pouring me a shot.

"It's 5, we aint leaving no time soon, you bout to be folded before you even get your hair done. You gone be the one blacking out." Shonda responded.

"Turn down for what?!" Dottie yelled skipping through the doorway.

"Right! I'm good boo." I said slapping my shot glass on the table after finishing my first shot. The table shook simultaneously with Shonda's head.

Dottie was the sweetheart. Our "peace keeper" is what we called her when she kept the peace in the house the days Shonda and I strong personalities clashed.

"What time are we leaving?" Dottie asked.
"I'm thinking about 10:30. Dave said he put our

names on the list so the least we can do is be on time." I responded.

"Cool. Shouts out to Dave fine ass." Shonda replied.

"Lay off my man Shonda before I have to fuck you up. I told you about that shit." I snapped back.

Shonda was always giving me shit when it came to Dave. One minute she acted like he was scum and the next she wanted to suck his cum.

"Trust me; I'm not the one laid up on your man." Shonda Responded.

"What's that supposed to mean?" I replied.

"What it sound like?" Shonda asked forcefully.

"Ay, y'all chill, y'all done got some devil juice in you and showing out already." Dottie interfered.

"Whatever, I'm chillin. That's Tina yamp ass." Replied Shonda.

"Ha." I laughed, poured another shot and headed to my room.

 Arguing with Shonda over my boyfriend was foolish. She called herself implying that Dave had been cheating but that was my first time hearing of that. I never been the type of female to take another female word for my man actions, but if he was doing his thang, I would get to the bottom of it.

After taking a nap and getting a few more shots in me, I was ready for the night. I got dressed, flat ironed my hair weave, rolled a few blunts, one for the club and the other for the ride to the club. It was definitely turn up time for me and my girls. Dottie and Shonda both looked like they belonged on the cover of the hottest urban model magazine, and myself? Well I had just stepped off the runway.

We pulled up to the club and finished pre-gaming. Blunts, and shots. I gave Dottie her three shots that she was limited to because it was her turn to drive.

"Hello?" I answered Dave's phone call.

"Baby, where you at? I thought you was going to be here early." Dave said.

" We are here, chillin in the parking lot. I'll be in there in a second." I responded.

"Alright, cool." He said and hung up the phone before saying bye.

"Rude bastard." I interjected after hanging the phone up and throwing it in my clutch.

Fifteen minutes later we were on the dance floor. Shonda was twerking up some dude and me and Dottie was twerking each other up. I had been calling Dave since I walked into the club and he had not answered one call. The music was loud and the walls were shaking, so I figured he did not hear his phone or feel the vibration.

After turning up on the dance floor for an hour straight, Shonda and I left Dottie on the dance floor dancing with some dude. My feet were starting to hurt and my buzz was starting to fade. Headed towards the bar, Shonda tapped my shoulder and pointed towards a smoke filled corner. I could see Dave talking to a woman. He was so close to her that you would think they were together, hell at least having sex. His right arm was over her left shoulder as they looked face to face. She stood on the wall and by the looks of things Dave was damn near standing on her.

I turned to look at Shonda, the look on her face mimicked the look on my face. We were both disgusted.

"So what you gonna do? Wanna go blow his spot up?" Shonda said.

She wanted to go confront Dave. I was not sure what I wanted to do at that point. As a woman, it just seemed beneath me to go confront him in front of a woman I knew nothing about. If he wanted her, he could have her but I was not about to give that woman a good laugh because my "boyfriend" wanted to make some dumb ass choices. Embarrassed or not, I would not be the butt of anyone's joke.

"No, I'm about to finish turning up and having fun with my girls. That situation can wait." I responded.

Dave was a wrap. Shonda knew all along. Maybe she had heard rumors, saw some fishy stuff or sensed he was trash. She knows me well enough to know that I would never believe anything she had to say about Dave without hardcore evidence, so she never brought it to my attention until today. Shonda was warning me to be aware of what could possibly happen tonight when she was fucking with me earlier. Real friends are hard to come by.

"Damn I wanted to see you cuss that muthafucka out. Maybe kick him in his balls or give that disgusting ass beard some jokes. Man make sure you give his little baby from some jokes to when you go at his cap." Shonda said laughing.

I laughed too. We headed towards the bar, ordered our drinks, finished them in less than 10 seconds, and found ourselves back on the dance floor, where we stayed the rest of the night. Guys were flocking to us and the cute girls wanted to know us. We exchanged numbers with some of the hot girls and invited a few of the guys over for the after party.

The DJ got on the mic and announced the last ten minutes. The lights came on and everybody started heading towards the door. I looked around for Dottie but she was nowhere in sight. Shonda pulled me towards the back exit doors after she noticed a few others exiting. I took my phone out to call Dottie when Shonda grabbed my phone out of my hands and pushed me towards Dave. He was standing on the side of the building with his arms around a woman. It was not the same woman from earlier.

The woman earlier was wearing the latest style of Louboutin; I was envious then and even more envious as I recalled the beautiful shoe. This time it was a familiar pair of shoes, some cheap shoes that I found more laughable than not.

"Dottie? What the fuck are you doing?" I said once I had a handle on the situation. The scenario was funny but I was not going to let her get away that easy.

"Tina, it's not what it look like. Dave asked me to talk so I came out here. Don't even trip about it." She said thinking of the quickest lie she could to save her ass.

"What the hell do y'all have to talk about?" I asked knowing damn well that they did not have shit to discuss.

"You baby. I wanted to do something nice for our anniversary and I knew Dottie would know." Dave responded.

"Save the bullshit Dave, I saw you inside the club hugged up with another chick. You just out here doing your thang I see." I replied.

"What other bitch was you hugged up on David?" Dottie interjected and asked as if she was his woman.

Like clockwork I grabbed her by her hair, punched her across her face, swung her to the ground, and kicked her with my heels. She tried to fight back but her 5 inch heels and mini dress helped me kick her ass even more. The tramp told on herself that quick. Girls lose their head when it comes to dick, women are usually two steps ahead just waiting for "go" moment.

Shonda flagged a cab down and we both got in. As we rode off Dave helped Dottie up, and I could tell they were still arguing.

"You gonna make her move out?" Shonda asked.

"No. She can stay as long as she want to and get her ass beat as long as she want to just the same." I responded.

"I feel you on that." Shonda Replied.

"You knew huh?" I asked.

"I sensed it, I didn't know for sure though. They were just too sneaky and close when he would come by the house. A few times I came to the house and he would be turning the corner or something. I would ask Dottie if he had come by, and she would always say no. Life taught me to just let things come to the light and I guess that's what happened tonight." She answered.

I sat back and took in everything I had just heard. The popular hip hop song "No New Friends" lyrics filled my mind as I zoned out. Tonight I would wash my hands with a close friend, and an ex-boyfriend.
"The after party still going right?" I asked Shonda.

"Hell yea, I was just about to ask you the same thing." She replied.

The party was still on, similar to the movement of life. Life would go on.

Love Lost

I once had a love like no other

Smelling love throughout the day

The loud tone that would keep me wide awake

I once had a love like

No other, so hurtful, and manipulative

The thought of it just makes me cringe

Just thinking about the knife fight

I once had a love so unusual and difficult

So heart breaking and humiliating

So dreadful, my heart aches

No coming back, 3 strikes

I once had a love so wonderful

Wonderful for the girl with no worth

For the girl with no hope

For the girl with no love

See I had a love that did not love me back

Oh how I long for that love

The only love that wouldn't love me back

How I long for that love

I just need you to take me back…

Single Wife Chronicles: Volume One

I jumped up and my leggings were soaked. I felt around the bed for a moment cursing myself for pissing in the bed at my old age. Then quickly I remembered my due date was in three days, my water had broken. I hopped out of the bed, well waddled and headed to the bathroom.

I felt around and sniffed like a 10 dollar whore on her way to turn her 1000thtrick. Yep, my water had broken.

"Brian!!!" I screamed to my boyfriend, as I looked at the bathroom clock.

It was 4 am. Brian was either up playing video games or watching some hardcore porn. He barely slept in the bedroom anymore due to my enormous uncomfortable stomach, which was protruding so much to the point I felt overcrowded in the bed with him.

I could hear Brian running up the stairs. He didn't scream in the house, it wasn't *in his character*,he reminded me at least once a day. For instance he would be outside, I'd call his name and he'd run all the way to where I was before uttering a word. He certainly was his own person which I most loved and appreciated.

"Girl do you know what time it is? You screaming at the top of your lungs like somebody died or something at 4 in the morning. Crazy ass."

"Ya momma crazy and my water broke. Get the bags by the door and put them in the car." I told him after listening to his rant about my screaming as if it was something new.

"Oh shit!" he screamed forgetting his whole argument.

"Stop screaming." I whispered trying to be funny.

Brian brought the good out of me no matter what situation we were in. He always made me feel like I was in high school all over again, that new young love, no worries, no problems, just us. Now that the baby was coming things would change a little. How much? Was the question that bounced around in my head from time to time. The baby had already kicked him out of the bed, what could possibly be next?

"You're real funny." He replied staring at me grinning.

I stared back at him taking in the visual. The man was all I ever wanted and more. His chocolate complexion, pearly whites, perfectly trimmed face, standing 6'2 at 245 lbs., the man was easily mistaken for a movie star, porn star, hell he could be a star in the sky the way he looked. Well at least to me.

"Hurry up and get the bags boy so we can go." I instructed.

"Got you, my son says he on his way." He replied as he started to move the bags to the car.

"He aint saying nothing yet." I said referring to my contractions. They hadn't started. I didn't know was this a bad thing or not.

Moments later I was in the Volkswagen headed to the hospital. Henry Ford was only 10 mins away and it only took Brian 5 mins to get there on this morning.

When I got settled in my room, the nurses prepped me. I hadn't dilated yet so they gave me medication through my IV. I started to feel contraction about and hour later.

Our parents arrived around the same time. Brian's mom Patty stood over in the corner not uttering a word. The woman never cared for me and the fact that Brian and I weren't married definitely bothered her. My parents tried their hardest to include her into the conversations and she withdrew just as much.

After 12 hrs of labor our beautiful, big eyed, bald head, chocolate drop was born at 9lbs and 10 ounces. Brian wouldn't put him down. Every time I turned around he was holding him or touching his face, anything to be close to his son.

We were ready to leave the hospital the next day. My labor had no complications and minimal tearing. I was a lucky one, Timmy made me a proud momma on his Birthday. Our parents had returned to help us get everything situated. My mom planned to stay the rest of the week with us to help with the baby. I wasn't sure why Brian mother had come, but I was glad she was starting to come around. Two days in a row was certainly progress for Patty.

My parents had taken the baby and my clothes to my mom's car while we waited for the discharge paperwork. Patty had stuck around to see us off I was quite impressed.

When I finally saw the nurse I grabbed my last belongings and made sure Timmy was bundled in his car seat. She handed Brian a piece of paper and me plenty of forms.

"Oh ma'am you can give him all of the paper work." I instructed the nurse.

"I'm sorry this has to go to you. I need your signature before you leave." She replied as she handed me the paperwork back.

I looked at the form and grew furious.

"I didn't ask for no blood test on my baby. I hope yall don't think I'm paying for this."

"Yes, you did and yes you are being charged Ms." She responded

"No she aint, I am." Replied Brian's mom.

"You did what?" Brian responded.

"From the conversation we had last week, I thought you would be okay with the blood test." Patty responded.

My phone began to buzz. It was my mother, they were waiting outside for us.

"What is she talking about?" I had turned to my complete attention to Brian.

"We were talking the other day and I agreed that it would make sense to have a blood test because it's not like we are married···"

"So we don't live together? You didn't think he was yours?" I cut him off mid-sentence I was

"Yeah we live together but we aint married. You wouldn't even name him after me.

"You said you were fine with naming him Timmy, this is the first I've heard of this!"

"Listen, you didn't let me finish. When you told me your water had broken all those thoughts went out of my head. I knew that Timothy is mines. I was tripping when I was thinking like that. I'm sorry."

"Well why did you go through with it?"

"Ma, told the nurse and when she asked me I just went with it." He responded.

"Oh. Okay. Well just go with your momma today." I told him. Brian wasn't the man that he led me to believe. He wasn't his own man.

"Yooo. Not today yo, not today. Let's just take the baby home and chill out."

"You know what. I think you should get your own place. Hell we aint married, we making babies, living together, but still needing blood test and other unnecessary bullshit."

"Well that's the smartest thing I done ever heard you say." Patty responded.

"You can get the hell away from me. I been trying to be nice to you and respectful, my parents have been trying to include you in and you bring around is negative energy. You're hateful and bitter. Move on Patty, find a man, take a vacation but please leave my relationship alone."

Patty just stood there. She didn't say a word. Her facial expression never changed. She was just quiet. The woman had just proved to be crazier than I knew.

No one said anything else to me. The nurse had been standing there the entire time getting a complete earful. She helped me get my things together and brought a wheelchair for me, helped me get into it and rolled me down the hall. Brian knew not to touch me or utter a single word to me. I was furious with him and only time would tell if our relationship would make it. He was definitely moving out of my house until he decided he was ready for marriage if ever.

"What took yall so long I been calling you and calling you? You were in the bathroom weren't you?" My mom started as I got to the car.

"No, I was having a conversation. I will tell you about it later." I responded making eye contact with Brian and his mom as they stood next to each other.

I climbed into the back seat as my father put Timothy on the other side. I went to close the door as Brian stopped it. He leaned in and gave me a kiss on the cheek.

"I will call you in the morning to see how you are feeling." He said sounding like he had lost his best friend and looking like a lost puppy.

"Okay." I responded.

"I love you." He replied.

I closed the door. I didn't want to tell him that I loved him too. It hurt so damn bad to have loved him at that moment. The disappointment was an enormous dagger.

I thought to myself *oh Timothy what other changes have you brought to my world?*

Baby Momma

You are the greatest

Through your pain you survive

With determination you provide

Baby Momma you are strong and resilient

Don't let them incriminate you

Don't let WIC hold you down…

Or up!

Stand my beautiful lady

Rise my beautiful woman

Search deep for that love you longed for

Find that love that put you here

That love you gave to that man

That love

That love

That love

Give it to the babies

Give it to your heart

Love yourself baby momma

Fight for yourself baby momma

Rise my beautiful woman

Stand my strong lady

Save our daughters!

What's Love Got to Do with It?

"Ant!" Sandy called from the other room.

"What Sandy damn? I'm playing the game." Ant yelled back.

"I just wanted to make sure that it was you I have not seen you in a few days." Sandy said in a low time.

"What you say? You come screaming and shit and then want to be all quiet. I can stand when you do that shit damn." Ant spat.

Sandy walked towards the other room.

"I said Hi." She said in an even lower tone.

"If you aint in there cooking some shit up we don't have shit to talk about." He explained.

Sandy turned around and walked towards the kitchen door. She was frustrated. It had been two months since Ant had anything decent to say to her, and then alone it was only because he wanted to have sex all of a sudden one day. She thought back to that day.

"Damn baby you know you looking good again. That baby weight almost off."

He had come home every day for a week straight that week. Sandy had thought it to be unfortunate but he was starting to act like the old Ant. He was coming home, playing with the kids and playing his video game. So when he climbed in bed with her for the fourth night in a row, something that he had not done in a while, she just fell into the arms of her lover of 9 years once again.

Ant made love to her that night. He kissed her in spots that sandy thought were forgotten. They connected for those twenty minutes.

The next morning he woke up, headed out for the day and did not return until two days later.

"I was at my momma house." Ant responded when he came home. The normal routine.

This time it was the same sad ass story. Ant had been gone for three days without any explanation and came home being rude and disrespectful like his normal self for the past 4 years.

Sandy started dating Ant when she turned 18. Fresh out of highschool, Ant moved her into his apartment. They had only dated for three months and Sandy knew that their lives would continue together forever. Sandy's mom did not like the idea of Ant and Sandy shacking up, mainly because of the five year age difference. Against her mother's wishes Sandy moved anyways.

Now she had to face the facts that her mother may have been right. Sandy had her own kids, and now saw what her mother once did –A manipulative coward of a man.

Sandy was fed up. She had packed her and the kid's things and planned to go to her mother's place.

Like a fairytale gone wrong, Sandy repeated the same question as she did before.

"Where have you been the last few days?" Sandy asked.

"I was at my momma house." Ant responded.

"I figured you were, the kids and I are going to my mom's for a few days. There is dinner on the stove for you if you want it and some is in the fridge wrapped up for tomorrow." Sandy said awaiting the huge blow up.

Ant never wanted her to leave the house, but he left for days at a time. When Ant found out that Sandy was not home he would call her cell phone numerous times, leaving sick messages, and followed up with text messages full of anger and deceit. The guilty conscience he had never allowed him to accept Sandy for the beautiful woman she was inside and out. Possibly the insecurities added to the constant disrespect Ant pushed on Sandy.

"Bet. Call me before you come home so I can make sure I cleaned up and shit." He responded.

Ant plopped down in my grandfather's old recliner, let the leg rest out and flicked the TV on. He clearly did not care. Ant's disrespect had reached an all-time high. Sandy could not help but to think that she had really chose a terrible man to fall in love with and father her kids.

Sandy went to the bedroom and through their boxes out of the window. Ant had not seen all of the boxes that were packed and she did not want to alarm him.

She bundled the girls up in their winter gear, gave them backpacks full of games and other entertainment, and they headed out the door.

"Momma, why we need all of this stuff if we just going to granny's for two days?" Sonya asked.

Sonya is Sandy and Ant's oldest daughter, also known as the brightest four year old ever.

"We will talk about that later. Get in the car." I responded.

Sandy knew that her daughters were growing up and did not want them to see her going through the foul things their father was putting her through.

She put her youngest daughter Briana in her car seat securely and checked Sonya to make sure she was secured. Once the boxes were in the trunk, Sandy closed the trunk, and climbed into the front seat of her old rusted out explorer. While driving away she took a look at their rental property and just the vision of Ant reassured her that she was making the best decision.

Self-Love, Better Love

Be confident in who you are.

Prepare yourself for greatness.

Leave the legacy behind

We are no longer objects to society

We are no longer Sara Baartman

We are no longer Solomon

We are people

Love yourself for who you are

Hate him in the mirror?

Change the reflection…

Fight for survival…

Know your history…

Be beautiful…

Be merciful…

Love

Love before hate